KEVIN HENKES

Kitten's First Full Moon

HOUGHTON MIFFLIN HARCOURT
School Publishers

For L, W, C & S

Acknowledgments

Kitten's First Full Moon by Kevin Henkes. Copyright © 2004 by Kevin Henkes. Reprinted by permission of HarperCollins Children's Books, a division of HarperCollins Publishers. "Drinking Fountain" from *Around and About* by Marchette Chute. Text copyright © 1957 (E.P. Dutton), renewed 1985 by Marchette Chute. Reprinted by permission of author. "Moon Boat," from *All Asleep* by Charlotte Pomerantz. Text copyright © 1984 by Charlotte Pomerantz. Reprinted by permission of HarperCollins Publishers. "The Puppy Chased the Sunbeam" from *Rode the Black Horse Far Away* by Ivy Eastwick. Copyright © 1960 by Abingdon Press. Reproduced by permission of Abingdon Press. "Silverly" from *Jelly Belly* by Dennis Lee. Reproduced by permission of Macmillan of Canada, a Division of Canada Publishing Co.

Credits

Illustration
32–33 Michael Garland; 34–35 Nathan Jarvis; 36–38 Jui Ishida.

Printed in China

Little Big Book ISBN: 978-0-547-88486-8
Big Book ISBN: 978-0-547-88478-3

7 8 9 10   0940   21 20 19 18 17 16 15 14

4500498655   A B C D E F G

Table of Contents

Paired Selections

It was Kitten's first full moon.
When she saw it, she thought,
There's a little bowl of milk in the sky.
And she wanted it.

So she closed her eyes
and stretched her neck
and opened her mouth and licked.

But Kitten only ended up
with a bug on her tongue.
Poor Kitten!

Still, there was the little bowl

of milk, just waiting.

So she pulled herself together
and wiggled her bottom
and sprang from the top step of the porch.

But Kitten only tumbled—
bumping her nose and banging her ear
and pinching her tail.
Poor Kitten!

Still, there was the little bowl

of milk, just waiting.

So she chased it—
down the sidewalk,
   through the garden,
      past the field,
         and by the pond.
But Kitten never seemed to get closer.
Poor Kitten!

Still, there was the little bowl

of milk, just waiting.

So she ran
to the tallest tree
she could find,
and she climbed
and climbed
and climbed
to the very top.

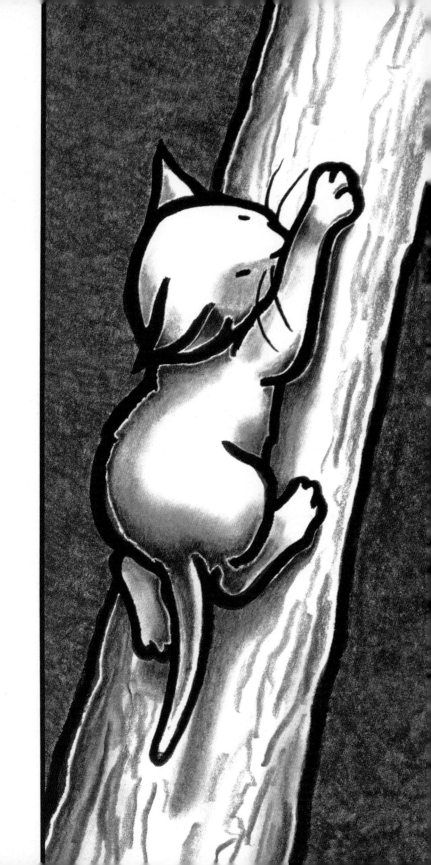

But Kitten
still couldn't reach
the bowl of milk,
and now she was
scared.
Poor Kitten!
What could she do?

Then, in the pond, Kitten saw
another bowl of milk.
And it was bigger.
What a night!

So she raced down the tree

and raced through the grass

and raced to the edge of the pond.

She leaped with all her might—

Poor Kitten!

She was wet and sad and tired and hungry.

So she went
back home—

and there was
a great big

bowl of milk

    on the porch,

just waiting for her.

Lucky Kitten!

Drinking Fountain

by Marchette Chute

When I climb up
To get a drink,
It doesn't work
The way you'd think.

I turn it up,
The water goes
And hits me right
Upon the nose.

I turn it down
To make it small
And don't get any
Drink at all.

32

33

The Puppy Chased the Sunbeam

by Ivy O. Eastwick

The puppy chased the sunbeam
all around the house—
he thought it was a bee,
or a little golden mouse;
he thought it was a spider
on a little silver string;
he thought it was a butterfly
or some such flying thing;
he thought—but oh! I cannot tell you
half the things he thought
as he chased the sparkling sunbeam
which—just—would—not—be—caught.

Silverly

by Dennis Lee

Silverly,
    Silverly,
Over the
    Trees
The moon drifts
    By on a
Runaway
    Breeze.

Dozily,
    Dozily,
Deep in her
    Bed,
A little girl
    Dreams with the
Moon in her
    Head.

Moon Boat

by Charlotte Pomerantz

Moon Boat, little, brave and bright,

Tossed upon the seas of night,

One day when I'm free to roam,

I'll climb aboard and steer you home.